Creative Writing
Anthology **2009**

Poetry

UEA Creative Writing Anthology 2009

Poetry

First published by Egg Box Publishing, 2009.

International © retained by individual authors.

This book is sold subject to the condition that it shall not, by way of trade or otherwise, be lent, resold, hired out, stored in a retrieval system, or otherwise circulated without the publisher's prior consent in any form of binding or cover other than that in which it is published and without a similar condition including this condition being imposed on the subsequent purchaser.

A CIP record for this book is available from the British Library.

UEA Creative Writing Anthology 2009 is typeset in Oranda 10.5pt on 13pt Leading.

Printed and bound by:
Biddles, Kings Lynn

Designed and typeset by:
Kettle of Fish Design, Norwich
www.kettleoffishdesign.com

Proofed by:
Sarah Gooderson

Distributed by:
Central Books

ISBN:
978-0955939945

Acknowledgements

UEA Creative Writing Anthology 2009

Thanks to the following for making this anthology possible: the Malcolm Bradbury Memorial Fund, the Centre for Creative and Performing Arts at the University of East Anglia and The School of Literature & Creative Writing at UEA in partnership with Egg Box Publishing.

We'd also like to thank the following people:

Trezza Azzopardi, Amit Chaudhuri, Jon Cook, Andrew Cowan, Mark Currie, Siân Evans, Giles Foden, Lavinia Greenlaw, Sarah Gooderson, Rachel Hore, Kathryn Hughes, Michael Lengsfield, Jean McNeil, Denise Riley, Rob Ritchie, Michèle Roberts, Val Striker, George Szirtes and Val Taylor.

Nathan Hamilton at Egg Box Publishing, and Catrin & Dylan Lloyd-Edwards at Kettle of Fish Design.

Editorial team:
Chris Astwood
Sue Healy
Alex Lewis
Jake Marcet
James Midgley
Philippa Stewart
Gareth Watkins
Jennifer Wong

UEA Creative Writing Anthology 2009

Contents

Foreword
Lavinia Greenlaw and George Szirtes i

Poetry
.... 8

Contributors
Chris Astwood 10
Penny Boxall 20
Krystalli Glyniadakis 28
James Midgley 38
Jenny Pagdin 48
Marisa Silva-Dunbar 56
Jennifer Wong 64
Samuel Zifchak 71

Foreword

by **Lavinia Greenlaw** and **George Szirtes**

We are sometimes asked by prospective applicants and students what kind of poet we are looking for. The answer is all kinds, any kind. As can be seen from the range of work included here, we have no house style. What we look for is an emerging voice, one that is distinctive enough for us to see how it might develop into something singular and new. We aim to help poets become themselves, not us or each other.

Chris Astwood's work spreads into landscape and community. It is less meditation than a sweeping survey of what makes experience local. The poems are generally set in his home, Bermuda. There is a sea-like movement in the longer poems, such as 'Watercolour', which seems to ripple with light, the language sophisticated but unliterary, the whole streetwise and racy while retaining an elegiac warmth we might associate with a poet like Derek Walcott in some moods. There is potential for real scale in Astwood's work. It would not be surprising to see him embark on something like a book-length poem.

Penny Boxall brings us an acute vision of the arrested moment, be it hesitation, transgression or uncertainty. Someone politely waits as she passes by before despatching a dying animal. Otters are perfectly described as both homely and peculiar: 'almost little dogs/and yet not dogs'. Her sestina 'Rush' shows how her poetry plays out in continual fine adjustments, unsettling and illuminating its subjects: 'but then you'll hear the shift/of falling silt, the settling of silver dust/through cracks in hidden stones, men sunk/under yards and yards of weight …'

Krystalli Glyniadakis maps the choreography of intimacy. Lovers fly in opposite directions in a reflection of their growing dislocation: 'And then you'll land/seventy-two miles north from where I left'. Her voices are passionate, restless and rootless: 'But first, first we must pass each other by.' Her poems fragment or marshal themselves according to the emotional tensions at play, and she has the imaginative confidence to reach for the synaesthetic and surreal, describing the smell of Istanbul as 'acrid, oblong/drooping to the ground in long lace curtains'.

There is both mystery and intelligence in James Midgley's work. It has a mature grasp of the darker aspects of life, but is fascinated by its sheer variety. He takes real risks, such as the monologue about Phineas Gage in 'Phineas survives', and explores dialogue and complex diction in 'The Sea Speaks with One Voice'. Each poem is conducted like a separate adventure, a matter of gaining confidence and mastery over that which is valuable but hard to define. 'The Clockmaker Assimilated by Clocks' ends with the lines: 'So I count what keeps me awake./I count what keeps me in the world.' It is commendably ambitious work, a restless kind of promise.

Jenny Pagdin's poems are sensuous, intimate, and formal works, windings of limbs and thoughts, in which she explores brief intervals and transitional states such as that of the birds bound for Africa in 'Elegy' or of a bird-like arrival in 'Migratory', but it is the closeness of human bodies that occupies the two longest poems here. Both are sestinas. The sestina is itself a winding form, coiling round and round the same six words, thinking, registering, and feeling in a meditative, serpentine fashion. Pagdin handles them with real grace, touching the subject lightly then moving on.

It is the cinematic sweep and detail of Marisa Silva-Dunbar's poems that first strike the reader, but they too are in transit. We pick up lives as they enter a location full of specifics. Here are places where things have happened or are about to happen. There is a sense of lives brutalised – the dead child in 'It Wasn't a Drive By', the sexual assault in 'It is easier to let these things happen', the father ripping the mother from the car in 'Leaving Town'. There are violences and violations, memories of growing up and friendships. The images are clear and sharp, the narrative always tight, rich and compulsive.

Jennifer Wong writes about the strange coherence of ancient and modern she sees in China today. Her poems resist neat juxtaposition, instead showing how past and present interact with equal force. She focuses on the persistence of ritual gesture: two women destroying a 'spirit doll' under a motorway flyover or the childhood enactment of diagnosis and cure ('Tom checked my tongue/with torch and ruler, pressed/a lemon fridge magnet onto my chest.'). There is persistence, too, in those who have been overwhelmed by history such as the mother who might 'take//like pills   each day.'

Samuel Zifchak's poems are lightly constructed, witty, anecdotal and seemingly offhand. Crafted out of a few details, an odd exchange or awkward encounter, they play out moments of painful or complex realisation without ever weighing themselves down. Zifchak is a technically dextrous poet who disarranges his lines to add further subtext. At the same time, he pursues clarity and economy. In 'I've become simple' he demonstrates (rather than lectures us on) the difficulty of being so: 'I've just/come to realise that I want people to/understand I want you to understand/as much as/is possible all that I want to say.'

There is no single style emerging from the work of the various poets here and that is all to the good. They bring with them their own angles to the world, their comprehension of how it behaves in language. They listen to each other and learn how things might be – sometimes how things might be better, sometimes just how they might be otherwise. They discuss their own work in a fully informed way, bringing with them a wide range of reading and reference. It is a pleasure to read their work.

LG and GS

UEA Creative Writing Anthology 2009

Poetry

UEA Creative Writing Anthology 2009

Chris Astwood
Penny Boxall
Krystalli Glyniadakis
James Midgley
Jenny Pagdin
Marisa Silva-Dunbar
Jennifer Wong
Samuel Zifchak

Chris Astwood

Old Man Pushing a Shopping Cart of Bottles Somerset, Bermuda
Watercolour Somerset, Bermuda
Sargasso
Down 'Squire' Somerset, Bermuda
Estimations of Pain at a South Shore Road Trail Head Warwick, Bermuda
Fever June Galesburg, IL

Old Man Pushing a Shopping Cart of Bottles Somerset, Bermuda

(rattling below)

His beard:

> brushes against the metal cage bounced on the uneven lane's studded asphalt;

> feels and has felt many dry and wet weathers since its last trim;

> swings like heavy Spanish moss when his eyes rummage the dark hibiscus;

> soaks itself daily in brown ales and chowder, dribbles of nose-blood and saliva;

> commands the palms at Mangrove Bay to stand unbent for its parade through the village.

(racket of drums)

Watercolour Somerset, Bermuda

"Made him push night"
Anthony McNeill THE KINGDOM OF MYTH/A Fable in 32 Lines

Under the purple wash
drown coastal cottages
       in the crepuscular hours
       when mosquitoes ready needles
for reverse injection
of vein-cooked haemoglobin –
       and up wave a few sprigs,
       tamarisk caught in the west wind
       that floats in the unthinkable
       mass of continental junk
              from the gulf stream, to where
              roots snarl up on sand and cement.

Cold turkey, he   shuffling
at doorsteps like   soft rain;

too polite to jump from kerbsides,
       he swallow whatever stuffing
       gets the sun to hurry up
       and climb the poincianas,
              dive and drown with the starfish
              he see each night – black water
              rippling on cracker-white faces.

Purple of bay grapes' ripe stink,
       of prickly pear whose trickster spikes
       draw like colours from the tongues
              and lips that bite too quickly
              into its juice-swollen promise,
the changing hour gives of
itself nothing more than moisture
and cock-cried warnings – almost

>   *almost almost   almost*
>   *not quite   not quite   not quite —*

that modulate and gargle
each time a sticker enters
the skin below the feathers.

Fly, fly, the needle ladies —
    insect eyes can detect
    the slightest twitch of a forearm
    or quickening of breath —
        straight for the thickest liquor's musk,
        the circulatory systems
of red veined orchids'
weak cellulose bodies — unused
to conditions at the edges,
        where rock faces and water spike
        out more with successive
        grumblings from heaven above,

the type of bodies destined
to root — half-sane — in hedges,
too bottom-stuck to be noticed
shaking under the high cane grass tides
    swaying, calm as seaweed garlands
    draped over the shoulders of waves,
        brushing their purple-blue skins
        and covering up the junk-blots —
the black tar lumps clotted
and working their way under the
meniscus to rock addled heads.

Crushed grape, he   veins thirsty
and fermented;   tongue leathered, he

    weighed limbs under slow-turning buds,
    lips with canker sores ripe

    as he taste the early sun,
the dread churn when the sea suds pink
and his body reek with bile
and brine – the stomach's
own mix of strong vinegar –

    Indigo road submerging him,
    mosquitoes twitch on the surface.

Chris Astwood

Sargasso

I sleep awake,   mouth full of salt,
limbs floating against you,   feel you wrap
around my ankle,   pull me into

your drift-knotted plaits: the only part
of you not fully sunken.

They've grown quick   these few years since,
wide as the sea   that swallowed you,
and their stink fills   these brine-soaked hills.

Night on the horizon: shark oil clouds
silence the birds   nothing on my mind
but scouring waves   keep me dreaming:

                                  Sargasso
shed and delivered   to the beach head,
twisted around lost plastics.

Down 'Squire' *Somerset, Bermuda*

We got half hot on Cockspur, fucked
up the bar mats and shot the shit
with rock burner Slew, who'd swore
off drinking, told his other 'rock star'

bredrin, *that shit'll fucking kill you*

(referring to the rum), and who hissed,
proud and stately, of his bush house,
chatting *shrew shree* front teeth,
parish elder now, since Lenny Flood –

the frazzle bearded alcoholic
poet who slept in an outhouse
down in the bamboo by Long Bay,
then went out back of Maxi Mart
for something – passed away,

and Slew wore it well when he turned
his grey, cracked head to me, and asked,

You know about Easter Sunday?
It's the day Jesus comes out and walks
down here to remind us that he's
always here with us, healing us,
you know?

Then bright headlights pulled up.

Slew counted up a stack of twos
and got up to buy himself a rock,
crossed the empty patio to the lot
like a man walking on water,

behind him at the bar: money
he would never see, and a light
less burning, less devouring.

Estimations of Pain at a South Shore Road Trail Head *Warwick, Bermuda*

In dry beach grass
hides the sharpest sticker,

a land urchin
the colour of chlorophyll.

Pulling the spine
from your foot's more painful
than treading it deeper.

Some stickers, we
ignore when they don't sting
bad enough, others

because their poison runs painless.

In the hours
of slowing traffic snarled up
above the trailheads,

how many drivers

will eye the descending sand paths

with the memory of a needle?

Chris Astwood

Fever June *Galesburg, IL*

Rain like this will miss the open window
every night until the misted prairie
manages to muster up its winds.

This second floor glows orange,
colour of the parking lot's tall lights,
hotter than their filaments.

On my flesh, I scratch away insomnia,
on yours, inscribe the shadows
with sweat on my fingernails.

Nothing comes stronger
than your breath, not the drunks
out keeping dry or drunk, not the bump

and hoot of freights rolling the nearby tracks
all night, not mosquitoes or the bean
stink from the coffee house below.

The creases in your skin flash behind
the passing cars. Our bikes, locked together
in the hall, knock against the wall

whenever this old building shivers,
brick sweat settling into chills
that rattle the scaffolding.

I will hold you beyond this fever June, weak
though I may be, skinny with hospital
corners folded at the edges of my eyes,

because I believe that, sleeping, you'll feel
my slow breaths, and remember:
this sick earth can sometimes be fair.

Born in Bermuda in 1984, **Chris Astwood** has been writing about his native Somerset Village for as long as he can remember. He holds a BA in Creative Writing from Knox College in Galesburg, IL, USA. His poems have appeared in *The Caribbean Writer*, *Catch*, *Iota*, *Other Poetry*, and *UM-UM*, and online at *The Smoking Poet* (www.thesmokingpoet.net) and *Underground Voices* (www.undergroundvoices.com).

Penny Boxall

Etiquette
Otter-hole
Everything I ate at Barton State Fair
Rush
Railway King
Three hares

Etiquette

August, and the air is thick with salt.
We walk the tree-lined avenues,
take comfort in the momentary shade.
Above the twisted-sinew roots
cement bulges. Crickets tune their strings.

The grid of streets makes right-turn
after right completion – it's on this stretch
that four are grouped round something
on the grass. A skunk, perhaps, or else
exotic moth – the teenagers

seem absorbed. A squirrel? It lies
fat as a pear, legs spoked as though
through gorging. The girl glances;
embarrassment clears her throat.
'I feel bad for him,' she says,

'with a broken back.' Of course:
her friend dangles the despatching mallet.
Seconds tick. They're waiting for our exit
at the corner, past the shielding trees.
All the way, I listen for a sound.

Otter-hole

Sag-bellied, hammocks of fur,
they curl in each other's
collarbones, plump with sleep.

They are almost little dogs,
and yet not dogs (their long
sad upper lips, their child's hands

balled on their tummies
and their feet, more than anything,
bootless). We eavesdrop through

this window on their burrow.
Our faces must be vast,
and still they snore – their dreams,

if they are dreaming, catching
in their throats.

Everything I ate at Barton State Fair

Even as we parked, settling dustily
in line with other cars on thirsting grass,
the blooming-onion stall was in full sight.
I'd been told about the delicious thick fists

of them, the crisped skin, the saucepot
balanced in their glib hearts. I was sold
before I ever found one, and here they were,
exploded globes the size of two cupped hands.

Next a candy apple, ripe as the world.
We cracked it, exposing fizzing white:
expecting nothing new, here we had the intense red
of its glazing, the high pitch of its taste.

Was it maple then? We had, certainly,
whipped maple creamies, soft as pillows,
and smooth mouthfuls of maple candyfloss,
tree-sweet; but that may have been after

the strange curried eggs bought from the man
who looked like a bearded egg – who had told
us in the first place about blooming-onions.
"If you like these," he'd said, his grey egg-beard

lolling to his waist, "you'll love bloomin' onions."
We'd stood in the Vermont barn, ogling possibilities.
Either way, we also had Hawaiian ice, and not
just one flavour – I had the sun and moon

of Georgia peach and green apple, and we sat
on benches, paint bubbled with old heat.
There were others, too – a sausage hot
with jalapenos, a rack of barbeque ribs –

but only so much I'm prepared to own.
There were other things at the fair.
We dodged the high hocks of oxen,
stroked the hens and rabbits through the mesh,

and on the way back averted our eyes from
the blooming-onions, to keep the memory sweet.

Rush

Let me tell you about things I've seen:
midday men lined toe-to-heel in dust
ruts, creaking with the dirt, their hands
all bitten to the bone and faces sunk,
all waiting, waiting; and the shift
from heat to sweating desert dusk

and then to particle-charged dusk
of underground. There's nothing to be seen
down there, but then you'll hear the shift
of falling silt, the settling of silver dust
through cracks in hidden stones, men sunk
under yards and yards of weight, their hands

metal-burnt. You should see their hands,
all red-raw, blistered in the campfire dusk.
We don't talk much to each other, sunk
in thought and aching. Things we've seen
by daylight are the same – the dust,
the heat, the prickly shrubs. Shift

work means we often come off shift
and see the next-day men, their hands
loose and off-guard, the skin of dust
not yet reached their faces. At dusk
we're ourselves caked. Have you seen
how thin a man can get, how sunk

into himself – the way his face is all sunk,
thin-skinned? I've watched them shift
from tanned lean daylight boys, seen
them turn to silver in the dark, their hands
pickaxed into shapes. But now, dusk
is on us, and you're thirsty from the dust

that's stuck all in your throat. That dust
will catch your voice, take it, sunk
in layers of dirt. I'll see you at dusk,
friend, once your awaited shift
is ended. Let me look at your hands.
You're not the strongest I have seen.

Railway King

'He had gout, he had drunken outcries, he even had a secret past, having fathered a child at 15 and fled his village in shame.'
The Observer, 2002

The Howsham houses lean their bricks in close
and talk amongst themselves. The bell shouts
from the ivy-creeping graveyard, makes known
its message of redemption – clears the air.
March ice is cracking on the ground.

Young George is not in church. Bonnets snap
to look behind, and blinker the view
of hymnals. George is not in church.
Hudson's there, his face obscured with his red
cloth-bound book; he's wearing something drab.

He'd sent a despatch rider with the dawn,
a procurement of apprenticeship, made fast
with shilling notes. His son's to be a draper
in the city, after everything's patched up.
That girl cost money, too, a bundle

of the stuff. He'll have pride enough,
he speculates, once he's made his way.
But now, he's in a fix. Over
the fields, the ingenious young man
is running trouser-less from town.

Three hares

The church, mile-distant, is slow waking.
It smells of powder, candle-wax,
the thick white smell of hymnals.
In a high-webbed corner, shadow-lit,
a trinity of hares is sharing just three ears
between them. They run their ring of wood,
legs crooked to fit.

Cook is in the steaming kitchen; the heft
of knife on wood is echoed by the slabs.
Along the table's length, the stripped limbs
lie. Quail and partridge nudge
soft secrets to each other, flesh pimpled
in the hot cave. The cabbage simmers fondly
on the stove, breathes scalding breath
against small windows. They stream from views
of constant snow — of blank sky falling into
lines of furrowed earth ploughed black
as liquorice.

Three rabbits — bare, and waiting
for the pie — lie ear-to-ear, each listening
to the next one's thoughts. They dream
of furlong fields, of hedgerows dark
as warrens.

Penny Boxall was born in Surrey in 1987 and grew up in rural Scotland and Yorkshire. She graduated from UEA with a degree in English Literature with Creative Writing in 2008.

Krystalli Glyniadakis

Leaving London on the occasion of your arrival
Young Mustafa Kemal arrives in Istanbul, 1899
Ode to a coffeeshop girl
[You came to me as if to say]
Bicycle stuck in snow
Scheherazade

Leaving London on the occasion of your arrival

Athens: British Standard Time + 2

At 7.30 a.m. (5.30 my time)
you took off from Athens International Airport
as I sat waiting placidly on a green, felt chair
at Gate 14, Gatwick North Terminal,
surrounded by the drone of Coke fridges.

I'd woken up around three
and by the time I'd bathed and dressed,
you were already checking-in.
You then bought your cup of ice-cold coffee
as I closed the black taxi door behind me with a thud
echoing in the chilly London night.

She took hold of both your passports,
planted a kiss on your cheek,
and handed you the day's paper,
black ink fading, smearing my fingers
as I read mine on the morning train.

At 7 a.m. BST (9 a.m. your time)
we reach our cruising altitude of thirty-eight thousand feet
past the Channel, into France.
Halfway to Paris, I see you crossing the Adriatic Sea,
Dalmatian isles lacing the surface of the water.
I read my book, turning the pages slowly,
counting away the minutes.
Our iPods pause;
you hear the stewardess enquiring
would that be chicken or vegetarian for you today?
You both have chicken.
I open my lonely bag of peanuts.

As you dance your *forlane* over Venice,
I respond with my jazzy Paris solo –
all flourish at both ends –
but mine is more sophisticated and yours is stiffer.
You'll see, you'll get there soon enough.

And then you'll land
seventy-two miles north from where I left,
having left me the sun
and the Athenian heat to keep me company
in your absence.
I've left you the cold, the rain, the morning fog;
after all, there's two of you,
you'll keep each other warm.

But first, first we must pass each other by.

And so we do, right here,
you glide right down below me
unaware of me, asleep upon her shoulder,
as I rhythmically grind my forehead on the window,
in alpine turbulence, trying to catch a glimpse of you flying by.

Krystalli Glyniadakis

How small you look in your metallic, white shell!
How gracefully you soar!
And how all this spreading whiteness below us
cannot contain the speed with which you dash right through my life.

Young Mustafa Kemal arrives in Istanbul, 1899

The city opens up before him blue and black.
The evening odd and unrepentant
scrambles onto the day's shoulder,
sticking its head above the minarets
and calling him to prayer.

The lamps strut their yellow stuff in military order.
From somewhere, the voice of the *salep* vendor
escapes the walls and rises up to meet
the muezzin's call, lamenting uniformity
in a city of religious clamour.

The sea sighs in the humid air, taut between two shores,
as if to force the continents together.
He feels its smell, acrid, oblong,
drooping to the ground in long, lace curtains,
sometimes touching him, sometimes not.

At the end of the Eminönü quay
the children drag their well-worn, leather sandals
along the dirty, cooling pavements.
His satchel moans from weight, his bearings
unaccustomed to sudden turns, departures.

He steps right in the city's steaming guts,
negotiates its cobbled entrails, *sokak*,
cadessi, *yol*, roof-hanging arteries and veins.
The city's imperial heart pumps blood
for all its subjects; the smell is sweet,
the tides have yet to turn.

Krystalli Glyniadakis

Yes, he must rest; so many miles upon him,
so many years ahead to fill his uniform.
And red, red, so much red, to quench
that crescent moon, that star.
But, for the time, the city opens up before him
blue and black, crimson and green,
seductive more than ever,
as happens always in the final act.

Young Mustafa Kemal arrives in Istanbul, 1899

Ode to a coffeeshop girl

Sweet chocolate   girl
                             k
s p   r n   l
     i   e d

hair wrinkles on your forehead.
blonde

You bloom   in
my mouth   begonias
                    froth
      on the windowsill. Kill-

ing time
in your coffeeshop
is   exquisite
      torture.   your
                        fingers –
     taste
     warm
     bread
     coffee
     beans
     just.
                    (roasted)
my voice
                caught in
                  my throat –

              inside of me.

I moan of cappuccinos.

Krystalli Glyniadakis

[You came to me as if to say]

You came to me as if to say
the day has run away with light
in tow and moons now rise and fall
on hollows low *and deal with it.*

And right beneath the evening sky
you came to me as if to sing
a midnight's lullaby of broken
skies and flat, hinged earth

stuck on a cardboard plane,
a postcard memory.
As if in vain my name you had
once carved upon your arm,

you came to me as if to ask
that I should hold the sun at bay
whilst you, more rough than ever,
paid night its ruthless, restless due

on someone else's wakeful bed –
the slow decay of years unlit,
the covers of the life you threw
away, for someone else's day.

Bicycle stuck in snow

The cold air smelled of falling in love.
Dismounted, you circled
around it, left it against the back wall
– chafed white wood –
and caught your breath;
chilled oxygen burning your lungs, your arms
still naked and fizzy, your fingers
dizzily crushing against the chain, your body
a stiff, resolute comb of happy flesh
under your flimsy T-shirt.
You opened the screen door,
walked in from the night
with the smell of early winter hanging
in the waning light
gently enveloping each thing
in its deep, metallic blueness.

Throughout the hours of darkness
you lay heavy with remembrance
of how you danced and how you fluttered
around each other's intellects,
gutted your histories to pieces,
abandoning regrets,
laughing the ice away.
You tossed and turned;
little by little, a pinch of salty marrow
by pinch of salty matter
had you swayed,
completing and rebelling
against each other's statements.
You kept awakening,
waiting for the light to break
so you could spin and dance again
on shifting ground.

Krystalli Glyniadakis

But now
your boots are shackled by the slush,
your ears no longer red, no longer callous,
they smell of warm animal skin and fur.
Your scabrous palms suggest some
cumbersome encounter
with splintered wood and filthy pockets,
breadcrumbs stuck deep within your nails
where all you wanted was her skin,
upon your fingertips her smell.
Unused you stand, like that soon-rusted scrap of metal.

Scheherazade

The nape of her neck
is so slender and vulnerable
I could snap her like a stick
between my fingers

    – maybe tomorrow

Krystalli Glyniadakis was born in Athens, Greece in 1979 and studied philosophy for seven years at the University of London before quitting her PhD and settling down with poetry. She translates Norwegian literature, paints, and harbours hopes of moving to Barcelona in the near future.

James Midgley

Incisions
Phineas survives
The Sea Speaks with One Voice
The Clockmaker Assimilated by Clocks
Insomnia
The Demise of Narcissus

Incisions

      Skin is skin – it takes a life
to get to the bottom of, so why
call it something else? The slide of my knife
will reveal the Adam's apple
as mere cartilage.

                    No, not mere –
and it is no sin trapped.
This is no confession. The screams
                are by-products.
But perhaps a lesson also: at first
the words were necessary –
      thyroid, trapezius, patella, sartorius,
      forehock and foot and hoof and flesh.
That layer of language lifts
      like the soft scroll
      between the shoulderblades.

                  Perhaps the words
are still necessary: I have scanned
the rhythm of these organs
gasping in light –
but the action is the syntax.

              And yes I was hasty
when I forbade comparison. There is
a metamorphosis
              but this is an unleaving,
a whittling down to pure operation.
One thing given up; another
                              retrieved.

Note: Phineas P. Gage (1823–1860) was a railroad construction foreman now remembered for his incredible survival of an accident which drove a large iron rod through his head, destroying one or both of his brain's frontal lobes, and for that injury's reported effects on his personality and social functioning – effects said to be so profound that friends saw him as 'no longer Gage.'

Phineas survives

but all the clouds are anvils on his back.
On my back – is it my back? I lean away
from my hands as if they are lizards.
Always those brown little lizards
would sun themselves in the parched air
by the tracks. Phineas summons rain
now, and here it pours. Its metal rounds
are one and a quarter inches in diameter.
Phineas drops to his knees and I reach
to pull him from the dirt,
a bridge leant down to drink its river,
but the lizards are under the hot sun and here
is the hot sun. We are a centre.
Thunder overhead, underhead, in the head.
Phin, you've dropped your hammer.
I move to scoop it from the ground
but it figures my nails wrong and thuds.
Nothing hurts. Sneezing
hurts, sometimes. I will find myself
scattered in the grass near a pair of boots,
sitting on a sleeper, inside the fireplace
that keeps the engine hurtling.
Small thoughts, you can come
out of hiding now. Goddamn it, Phin, goddamn.
And that too: Phineas has been god,
genius of a leaking faucet. To be expected.

In one of my memories I am looking at a skull
in a museum. In another I am a black eel
made of metal, ready to be thrown.
Phin, I say, Phin, come out of the tunnel, but
I cannot: speak or come out of the tunnel.
Some archer has drawn back my spine – released.

The Sea Speaks with One Voice

for three voices

Fisherman
        I've wondered at the somersaults of fish
           the repeated shoals   my boat loning the ocean
        A minnow is all twiddly bones
        What binds them together?   Is it

Sailor
        the sea: I want to name every ripple every wave
        all froth and maelstrom   This is the neglected
           and inconstant garden   I could be
        the first   Here I will name me Adam under the stars

Lighthouse Keeper
        I threw them there   tiny white snowdrops
        Threw those little cinders with the lamp I lit
        at the start of days   I was first

Sailor
        No I

Fisherman
        I grumbled up such a glut of fish   I gave them away
           I let their ghosts slip down streets   rainstorms
        on the mongers' windows   trotting cats gulping down
        their own mewls   I won't know what I fed   only

Sailor
        what you kill?   I know something of minnows
        like yourself   I take the boat out alone   no need
        for light or company

Lighthouse Keeper
>> Always a need for light   What is the world without it
>> the sea reduced to a scared animal
>> an intake of breath?   I snore louder   See
>> the poppies in the sundown sky?   You will know
>> something of what runs in my blood   It is the moon

Fisherman
>> The red moon?   I have wondered about it and the fish
>> that rise to glimpse it   that rise into it
>> despite the sniping birds

The Clockmaker Assimilated by Clocks

I counted what kept me awake –
a cockerel stamping the earth a mile away;
my own arrhythmic pulse.

The gold coins of pendulums rolled
over my eyes, rolled off again.

My cramped hands stabbed,
as a wader might dip its beak to taste
for what has not died or disintegrated.
Every river kills its fish
with the hammer and squeeze of current.

The insomniac cog in the sky turns. I stand
at the centre of moonlight's chronograph.

Hunched at a lamp where flies are brittling,
I link metal veins with a soldering iron
and count what keeps me awake.

The luminous paints make my fingers shudder
but the minute hand thumps and thumps its bass.

My eye adjusts its million faculties,
hones to the second's unanxious twitch.

My ear admits this cabinet's
acoustic of unending rain.

So I count what keeps me awake.
I count what keeps me in the world.

Insomnia

That which you call oblivion —
it was a door and breath the key.
Did you spot the cottage, as I did?
The place we all lived for a time
in monochrome, our bodies
wood shavings in a constant light.
The wind would not take us
anywhere. We had no memory
beyond that house of reason,
the one tree
bulging with every kind of fruit.
But I remember this —
every night the birds
would think it dawn, their tiny heads
suffused with light
like plumaged bulbs. They sang.
And our father hurled one stone,
the only stone, a perfect shot.
That stunned creature
swelled, up there on the roof.
It is still growing.
Look: it is filling up the sky.

The Demise of Narcissus

>   *De quo consultus, an esset*
> *tempora maturae visurus longa senectae,*
> *fatidicus vates "si se non noverit" inquit.*
> **Ovid** *Metamorphoses*

Dear Lord   what is light
if not form   love if not light?

At wood's edge a stag nudges free
   of the sun
              into the blind gaps between trees.
But no annihilation of self.

                  Dear Lord
  I am wary of water   my wrists bleed
the treacle of pines.
              I am wary of rain's
goldrush into fields
                my scattered teeth
   the sky almost reaching
                  into my head.

         But no annihilation of self. No
use looking in mirrors
                for loved ones
looking for loved ones
            in ice
   under false pretences.
                Look
   the well imprisons the clouds.
                Look
at the aura of buttercups
              nuzzling the chin.
Dear Lord   how did I see

in the quaked puddle   and
    what did I see?
                You surprised
                You butter-loving
                You building a shrine

of flowers
        and burning it.

Translation of the Epigraph: Narcissus's mother asked the seer Tiresias whether her son would lead a long and healthy life, to which he replied, "If he does not come to know himself."

James Midgley was born in Windsor in 1986. His poems have appeared in journals such as *Agenda*, *Iota*, *Magma*, *The Rialto*, *Stand* and *The Warwick Review*. In 2008 he received an Eric Gregory Award from the Society of Authors. He edits the literary journal *Mimesis* (www.mimesispoetry.com).

Jenny Pagdin

Occlusion
Biology
Elegy
You put your clothes back on
In worrying, I miss the peace
Migratory

Occlusion

Where were the first beating insect wings?
The first time we met your tweed had shocked me.
This curse of perception: although I disguised it
And you put on a front, I knew you'd seen.
But you, in a low that idolised politeness,
Clung to anything resembling warmth –
Was it at that time? When you couldn't speak
Through the depression, and I raked dry words
From hard chalk – is that when the light split
In all its colours for you, plated the grey?

Hearing you loved me, I was overcast,
Hoping the poem you folded over and over
Was nothing, although it spoke of marriage
And ordered gardens; wanting to believe
You shivered for the late September weather
And not for what you thought you read in me.
We know, although they forecast every day,
Tomorrow's hardly ever any different;
These systems change so imperceptibly
That when the weather breaks we'll not know why.

Biology

It feels like touching a child in the womb, here where
My hands meet you in the dark bath, and you start
With a drawn-in frisson when I touch you there,
Fall swiftly apart.

You called them your twin souls, your spiritual heart,
It's more than a joke now. These soft eggs share
Enough to repopulate the Earth, to impart

All that's instinctive. It's more than I can bear:
Cradle your microcosms – we'll have no part
In the worlds where our sons grow, incubate, flare,
Fall swiftly apart.

Elegy

What little light is left now, dismal glare,
Squats under a sodden tent. Most birds are bound
For Africa; those staying skim the ground
And circle like a mobile, beating air
In hopes to still it. These last months will wear
Their wings to tatters, till they run aground
On sedge-pale brushwood, and the frosts compound
A glass-bead harvest, and they'll be unaware.

Difficult not to feel something amiss:
The branches clumped together at the top
Like dirty feathers, are weighing me with grief.
Where do you gaze, wing hoverer? I'll watch all this
Till my unfinished net of words can drop
Over the county like a skeletal leaf.

You put your clothes back on

You put your clothes back on, close
The door to keep the room warm,
Heat the UHT for cocoa, toast my last piece
Of bread. You must have read
My thoughts wandering in the earlier part
And later we don't play, just lie and loosely touch,

We lie in the dark and where our toes touch
It's warm and still, and I feel very close
To you here in the darkness, almost part
Of the beating under me, in this our warm
Shared breath. It's too late to read.
We lie and let our bodies drop in peace.

Then after you've plundered every last piece

Of clothing, and I'm begging you to touch
Me here please, where it's marked in red
(You're doing great now and I'm very close)
Then all of it happens and I feel myself warm
To you more now, and I cannot bear to part.

And afterwards you say it's time to part
Again, and leave me, and an exhausted peace
Undoes my tears – pain dropping into warm
Water. I tighten to your ghost-limb touch,
Trying to keep the feeling close,
Then trying to sleep / trying to read

To read,

'part ...
        close ...
                peace ...
                        touch ...
                                warm ... '

Jenny Pagdin

And still, where our lips are so very warm,
And here where my fingers speak, can you read
Me asking if it's love, from the top side of our touch?
Is the feeling that carries across the joining part
Of our hands the same – through this piece
Here on the edge of your palm? And could we be nearer? How close?

(Maybe, however warm our fingers, part
Of each stays still unread, a piece
Of the gap no stitch or touch can close.)

In worrying, I miss the peace

In worrying, I miss the peace,
Turning over and over how the
Last time could have been better, how little I am sure of
Anything, with you: still
Unsure I like the quality of your voice
And thinking that my love may be too small.

Keeping everything small:
Disturbing myself from any peace
With this diminutive inner voice
Which stops me hearing the
Stuff, though very beautiful still,
With which you're kissing one of

My legs. It's really not the whole of
Me, thank goodness, this small
Voice of sabotage. Still
I know – even at its loudest – I'll come back to hearing peace
As soon as I'm quiet enough for the
Shell-like silence to drown this bugging voice.

I hear now the affection in your voice,
My love, and I'm glad of
You. In time I'll come to register all the
Beautiful things that happen (however small
Or close) and I'll be quiet enough for peace.
At least we're hugging still,

Lying very still
In the duvet darkness, your kiss here, your voice:
I try to create some peace
Although this is not one of
The things I planned for, and although in this small
Space we haven't yet played out all the

Jenny Pagdin

Things we might want to do and the
Bits we might yet say. Still
If you're feeling love, however small,
It's best to give it voice:
There aren't that many things of
So much value — maybe peace

(— If that is what we should call the barely heard voice
We find still waiting here, the blank sound of
This small and disappointing peace.)

Migratory

What could you know of those readjustments,
The preening a hard surface out of the air
That we could spread our wingbones on and glide
In a single movement over the ocean?

Through four dark dawns and days of hunger sickness
We dragged our waste-clogged feathers, though strings of rain
Fettered us, and we sometimes had to fight
To keep still as the headwind drove us backwards.

Fearing the winter we brought, you tried to trick us:
Blotted the stars out with those orange lines
Of lights which set us off our course
So that we had to trust our older magnet sense

And feel for landings in the dimming grey
– And we were flailing, for our fathers had never been here,
Skimming the surface and the gloomy shadows.
We! Who had been as the clouds and the wind moving through them!

Sometimes we came down on estuaries,
On mudflats and marshes rich with teeming worms,
Or on the stubble fields of your coastal farms
And fed on your winter grain and the late sugar beets.

Ever watchful, we crossed the leathering currents
With the curse of a new winter in our V-shaped wake.
But we'll not feed here again; we are going west
And leave these exhausted lands beneath our skein.

Jenny Pagdin graduated in English from Oxford University in 2000. She lives in Norwich where she works as a charity fundraiser. Her poetry has appeared in magazines including *Agenda*, *The Frogmore Papers*, *Nthposition* and the Selfridges magazine.

Marisa Silva-Dunbar

Leaving Town
It Wasn't a Drive By
It is easier to let these things happen
Love Rivals
After Three Years
Family Lies

Leaving Town

In early summer we packed up
your olive green jeep, headed through
mountains to the mining town
where gypsies gathered once a year.

Speeding down traditional dusty roads
of the canyon – sun in its fall,
we passed land dotted with sagebrush.

After we drove by the motorcycle diner you slammed
the breaks, and parked overlooking the baseball field,
littered with tie-dyed tents and bonfires.

Gulping down soda, feet pressed to the windshield
making our own constellations with prints,
you talked about never going home,
taking the highway east – forgetting
your parent's gambling debt,
the man who didn't marry you out of high school.

Now, I think about the two a.m. call,
you wandering through the damp park
crying down the phone – bolting
after your dad ripped your mom
from the car, fists meet face
when you tried to grab her hand.

Weeks later I waited for news,
sightings of you parked on the side of the road
Picking up the phone, your voice still hangs
on the line.

Marisa Silva-Dunbar

It Wasn't a Drive By

'There was a deliberate attempt to cover up what happened,'
Police Chief Ray Schultz said. 'They disrespected the death
of this baby.'
Albuquerque Journal, November, 2007

Monday afternoon, the house is booming,
Law and Order on the tube, the blaring
horns of *Straight Outta Compton*.

You can hear his laugh in the front room,
echoing still. You wonder if he cried after,
screamed maybe – for you.

The hall is littered with drywall,
the tube of toothpaste used to fill
in the holes, the shell casings

scattered on the floor. You imagine
hot metal bursting through skin.
The rug now smudged

with soap and blood reminds you
of his yellow shirt stained earlier
this morning with grape jelly and fruit punch.

You think of his body on the lawn
with toy cars, his brown skin
cutting through the grass.

They carried him there after firing
the round, 'it was an accident.' You can see
the curl of his dad's finger on the trigger.

It is easier to let these things happen

I don't like to watch the fast motion of your hand
up and down. I look away into the black room.

You remind me of the moments in sophomore bio,
when the teacher with coke-bottle glasses would leave the class.
The boys next to me would crowd too close, one shoving
his fingers up my skirt, the other clamping his sweaty
salty hand over my mouth.

In the back no one said anything,
the jars of baby pigs and frogs filled their throats.

Love Rivals

Outside we were a photo and its negative
like *Violet & Claire*, but we didn't terrorize
LA in the hazy sunsets, or get lost
in Joshua Tree at dusk.
We weren't a gunmetal Hummer,
glitter pink pixie dust, or Poison
Ruby nail polish dripping
onto pavement near pools.

We were different strands
of colored Christmas lights, hanging
in a teeny-bopper's room,
flashing at different speeds.

We took moments from each other.
Your first date sprawled
on the blue bench, I an unwilling guest,
trying to wind my words
into yours, a copper coil
strangling your conversation.

You stole kisses from the boy
I wanted, butterfly lashes fluttering
when he'd smile down at you.

We were pieces in the same game,
neither of us became his.
You and I both discarded,
like jacarandas in the desert,
children when it happened.

After Three Years

I

Our knees pressed together
you talk about the east coast truck driver,
how you left after three years
of waiting and listening to the sounds
of beer bottles collecting on the table.

We could be different, spend Friday
nights dancing to Tito Puente in neon clubs,
collecting the Miami heat with our skin
until the sun spreads into Matheson Hammocks.

II

You write from home near the War Zone,
mention your new lover and her fondness
of knives, how she likes tracing your Arabic
tattoos after soaking in the tub
and too many margaritas.

You say we were like Warhol and his long-legged
muse, I was just your superstar of '05
jumping to the sparkle of the spinning
disco ball in the small uptown apartment.

III

It was no fairy tale, three years waiting for you
by spring, sighing over boys at the counter,
while you camouflaged into suburban life.
No numbers, letters – no trace of you remains.

Marisa Silva-Dunbar

Life is complete – baby on your knee,
husband home, linens fresh blue and palms.
Glittery martini glass against your plum
lips, husky voice you used to bank on, silent.

Family Lies

Your mama's been feeding
you oleander blossoms again,

like she did when your cheeks spilled over
your rosy face, and you were bare bottomed
on the linoleum floor.

Such a sweet mama let the phone ring
when Daddy would call, tell you to watch
the colors stream across the TV screen
while placing Cheerios on your tongue.

After she dressed you in Raggedy Ann overalls
her new man took you for afternoons
in the park on days Papa was supposed to stop by –

driving up from desert into the crisp Michigan fall.
Your mom only gave him an hour with you in
the fluorescent light of a Mickey D's. Crying
most of the time, you now forget those evenings.

You only remember one day at the lake and all his
faux pas as a father. You claim the phone stayed silent,
for three years, until I came along.

You say these things don't matter much anymore,
worry that your mother's words will burn away like
pineapple resting too long on your tongue.

Marisa Silva-Dunbar is a native New Mexican. Originally an Anthropology major, she switched to Creative Writing after taking a poetry workshop as a freshman. She misses green chile and well-made coffee.

Jennifer Wong

Nanluoguxiang
Menace
Golden
Play
Daylight Saving
Whole

Nanluoguxiang

They say we don't know what's good anymore, what with
The old Beijing fading fading,
How priceless that heroic dignity, beauty
Of a preserved world.

At the foot of the Forbidden City
The lowly alleyway spreads like a dream,
Peppered with *hutong* names of a simpler life:
Chrysanthemum, rain and hats
Cotton, beans, and black sesame.

At Zha Zha café young heads
Hunch over a game of cards,
Smoke a fag or two,
The dim light and whirling fan continue.
In the corner a sensuous girl
Flips languidly through the evening post,
Her black waterfall hair spread
On the red Shanghai Tang floral print sofa.
The backpacker in transit
Types an email to his beloved,
WIFI signal on his MacBook flashing, flashing.

Lao Beijing you don't know anymore,
Sadly the travellers lamented,
Weeping for a better time, a better people they never saw.
In the *hutong* the Beijing ancient in a white undervest
Walks on, drinking *douzi*, his granddaughter
In front, skipping rope.

Night deepens. A local time savoured.

The grocer outside Central Academy of Drama
Goes on to sell his fresh plums and apricots,
Unwary of the Zhang Ziyis of his time
Coming and going
Under the radius of light,
That swinging low wattage bulb of his booth.

Menace

Each time I passed by the underside
of Gooseneck Flyover, I stared
at what they thought they were doing,
two women dealing blows to a spirit doll,
each shoe-thud or needle-jab
landing precisely where it was meant.
There was no mistaking
The dark fates they willed.

In the flickering shadows the white tiger lurked,
baring its paper fangs. The red candles gulped.
Satisfied, they told one another, with glazed eyes,
'at last justice has been served.'
All of us shuffled past the women
as if too much in a hurry to notice
or interfere with what happened.

Golden

Brimmed with night thoughts, a mother
prepares her patterned *qipao*
for next morning's tea ritual.

On wedding's eve, a blessed ancient
sings and runs a bright comb's teeth
through the young one's sweeping hair.

Piety burns in a leaping candle flame.
The moon is perfect. The bride

eagers for the morning
to claim him and his surname.

There will be thirty-three tables
that fill a banquet hall, coconut shells
hand-painted with double happiness,
pleasure of a strange bed
and a bold house waiting.

Play

As usual a few of us would make an eager queue.
Perched on a wooden bench, Tom checked my tongue
with torch and ruler, pressed
a lemon fridge magnet onto my chest.
Anna doled out for me two jelly beans:
proven remedy for a broken heart.

Helen claimed to suffer
from bouts of loneliness and strange dreams.
She demanded the syringe.
Anna injected a mechanical pencil
into Helen's flabby arm,
dabbed it with a rubber to remove the pain.
'Okay. Go home now
and no more cake for two days.'
Adam moaned about homework
and pains of growing up.
He got a small cup of apple concoction.
'Drink this, and you will feel better.'

On the other side of the playground
boys from another class hardly cared
for our game, too busy with their bullying
or gunning down birds with water pistols.

Daylight Saving

Today we put our clocks back
an hour for winter
while the sun continues its journey
southward-facing.

You may stay the night
longer than usual, less

time for your legitimate home,
where you keep a clean wardrobe of smart suits
and half-hearted promises.

It's hard to say goodbye
to old summer time.
We all want our own, best-kept backyard gardens
sweet with basil, bleeding hearts and foxgloves.

Where has the lost hour gone, has it made its way
to Antarctica – a round-the-clock summer –
or to an unremarkable woman?

They say going back an hour
is good for the heart, but gives too much carbon.

All through the night, the shiny face
of your one and only home-going watch
laughs at my ignorance.

Jennifer Wong

Whole

In late afternoon light you
scrape off its scales and gills
under cold running water,

empty its stomach,
swim bladder, rinse
the bloody slime, then
part, divide

bone and bright flesh
with precision.
The blade gleams

perpendicular.
Mother, it's you

I wish, I wish.
Mother, you take

like pills   each day,
will never lose

this tiled dream you play
house and rule.

Jennifer Wong was born and grew up in Hong Kong. Her poems have appeared in journals including *Aesthetica*, *Cha*, *Coffeehouse Poetry*, *Dimsum*, *Iota*, *The New Writer* and *The Reader*. Her poetry collection, *Summer Cicadas*, was published by Chameleon Press. She started writing poetry when she read English at Oxford.

Samuel Zifchak

Blind Spot
Grandma
I've become simple
Impasse
Barcelona
Drunk

Blind Spot

you take everything in 2s
lovers pills stairs thrills
                      look you say
laughing as the world kaleidoscopes
beyond comprehension   *look*
  you say as the pendulum collides
reducing grandfather to smithereens (that
took _____! screams the composer of
time)   *look*
  you cry pointing blindly at your chest.
    What? I gawk and glare at you.
Look. Desperate now. Pleading. What?
    I strip you. Examine and paw you.
        Hurt you. Desert you.
                      What?

Grandma

In a car with a fiery lesbian
    and her deaf girlfriend
to visit my grandmother who,
in the throes of dementia, often
mistakes me for the brother of
myself
    we are listening to trance
  because Mel can feel the vibrations
and the Australian scenery flashes by:
dried grass   gravel   eucalyptus   dust
   Ember is lost and swears at nothing.

                  Everything swears back.

I've become simple

        in my 20s
I once would spend
hours thinking of the perfect
metaphor to describe the way
  the bitter English sun shone
     through our window and
       glanced off your skin
  but these days it feels almost trite
I hope you don't mind this unpoetic
     approach to poetry I've just
  come to realise that I want people to
understand I want you to understand
       as much as
  is possible all that I want to say.

Impasse

I feel selfish 'cos you feel
much more towards me than I you
(or more than I am willing to)
and suddenly it's such a deal
that our views match in every way
or, at least, mine matches yours,
for yours, being higher up, deplores
my lower outlook's every say.
But damn it! I can't change for you:
I can't flick on the feeling switch
and frankly, you'd be quite a bitch
to ask me: 'make what's not come true'

                        but I love you. Does that not count
                           in your discussion of amount?

Barcelona

I have a boyfriend
she says and slips my hand
           under her shirt
             how did we end
up here on her Barcelonan balcony
smoking cigarettes like they were addictive
(I smoke because I don't want to be
one of those non-smokers) I see us reflected
in glass in the next apartment building in the
water which I splash my face with after shaving
and I ask myself as I lie down once more
helpless to her touch 'what am I doing here?'

Drunk

She shoots back her 5th scotch (straightnoicethankyou)
and continues: '   ...   miserable. All of them.
Writing about broken hearts and could-have-beens and
everlasting love   where are the poets of action, Sam?'
I swirl the contents of my glass and realise I don't even
                         know what I'm drinking anymore.

Samuel Zifchak has an Australian passport but has been travelling so long he is unsure of what that actually means. He started writing at a very young age (mostly about his cat) and has been writing ever since. He is, in his own words, lost, but continually, perpetually being found.